The City
and
the Country

 HEINLE
CENGAGE Learning

 Young & Son
Global, Inc.

Do you live in the city or the country?

Contents

the city

subway

indoors

outdoors

tractor

the country

The City and the Country

People live in the city or in the country. There are many streets and buildings in the city.

The country is different.
There are many fields and trees
in the country.

Where People Live

In the city, people live in houses or apartment buildings.
People live close together.

In the country, people live in houses and on farms.

People live far apart from each other.

How People Travel

People in the city drive cars. They also take taxis and the subway.

The subway train travels underground.

People in the country drive cars, too.

They also drive tractors and trucks.

These children are riding in a tractor.

Where People Work

In the city, people work in offices and use computers.
They work indoors.

Office workers use computers.

On a farm, people raise animals and grow their own vegetables. They work outdoors.

This farmer is holding some carrots.

How are the city and the country different?

the city	the country

Where We Live

People live, work, and play,
In very different places.
You live in the city,
You live in the city,
You live in the city,
And we live in the country!

People live, work, and play,
In very different places.
You live in the city,
You live in the city,
You live in the city,
And we live in the country!

Index